Basketball

Basketball Made Easy

Beginner and Expert Strategies For Becoming A Better Basketball Player

By Ace McCloud
Copyright © 2015

Disclaimer

The information provided in this book is designed to provide helpful information on the subjects discussed. This book is not meant to be used, nor should it be used, to diagnose or treat any medical condition. For diagnosis or treatment of any medical problem, consult your own physician. The publisher and author are not responsible for any specific health or allergy needs that may require medical supervision and are not liable for any damages or negative consequences from any treatment, action, application or preparation, to any person reading or following the information in this book. Any references included are provided for informational purposes only. Readers should be aware that any websites or links listed in this book may change.

Table of Contents

Introduction 6
Chapter 1: Basketball Basics 8
Chapter 2: Stretching and Warm-Up Techniques 13
Chapter 3: Improving Your Game 16
Chapter 4: Basketball Strength Training 27
Chapter 5: Diet and Nutrition for Basketball Players 37
Chapter 6: Building Mental Strength 42
Conclusion 53
My Other Books and Audio Books 54

Be sure to check out my website for all my Books and Audio books.

www.AcesEbooks.com

Introduction

I want to thank you and congratulate you for buying the book, "Basketball: Basketball Made Easy: Beginner and Expert Strategies for Becoming a Better Basketball Player."

Basketball is an amazing sport. Internationally recognized, the game is enjoyed by all ages all around the world. The object of basketball is for players to score points against each other's team by getting the ball into the hoop on the other team's end of the court.

The game was originally created in 1891 by a pastor in training named Jim Naismith. Naismith was assigned to teach a physical education class at the YMCA and was tasked with inventing a new indoor game to occupy a group of restless young men during the winter months. He quickly came up with a game plan that involved a simple set of thirteen rules. While today's "basket" is in reality a short net hung from a metal hoop, the game was first played using peach baskets, one at each end of a gymnasium, tied up to a bottom rung of a balcony. Naismith's invention was an immediate hit; basketball, as it was dubbed from the start, quickly spread from YMCA to YMCA across the country.

The concept soon was adopted by colleges, where players formed leagues. The game grew in popularity around the world to the point where it was declared an Olympic sport in 1936. The first professional game was played in 1898, but teams arose and folded for decades before stabilizing somewhat with the establishment of the National Basketball Association in 1945.

Basketball is an exciting and dynamic game. Unlike American football, the players adopt offensive and defensive roles as needed. The game is very easy to learn and practice. All you need is a ball and a hoop.

The sport has known many influential players throughout the years such as Michael Jordan, Magic Johnson, Kareem Abdul-Jabbar, LeBron James, Wilt Chamberlain, Larry Bird and many more. These players have brought increasing levels of speed and skill to the game, adding to its excitement and inspiring generations of younger players.

With enough practice, dedication, and motivation, you too can give yourself a fair shot at becoming a great player. This book contains proven steps and strategies to help you become a better basketball player. Beginners will discover valuable information, including the basic rules of the game, the types of players and their positions, the required gear, and essential basketball terminology. After familiarizing yourself with the game, you will move on and join the more experienced players in discovering the best advanced techniques for becoming a better basketball player.

stretching and warm-up techniques to prepare yourself for practices, workouts and competitions.

The bulk of this book contains some of some of the best tips and strategies to strengthen your physical abilities and sharpen your technical skills. Here you will discover some of the best strength and agility training exercises that will help you build your power, endurance, and explosiveness on the court. You will also learn proper warmup and stretching routines that will help you perform better and lessen your chances of injury. Then you will discover some top-rated diet and nutritional tips to help you keep your body energized and performing at its peak. Finally, you will discover some top mental techniques and psychological strategies that will supplement your physical prowess to make you into a powerful, smart and well-rounded athlete!

Chapter 1: Basketball Basics

How the Game Works

Basketball is a fast-paced, dynamic sport that requires close teamwork. Each team has five players on the court at any given time. A basket is suspended ten feet above ground at each end of the playing court. Each team is assigned a basket to guard against its opponents.

The object of the game is for the team members to work together to move the ball down the court and into their opponent's basket. Depending on a player's distance from the basket, sinking the ball through the hoop is worth either two or three points. After one team has made a basket, the ball is turned over to the opposing team.

Each game is divided into four quarters, the length of which depends on the level of play. Professional quarters last twelve minutes. College games have ten-minute quarters and in high school the quarters are eight minutes long

After the second quarter, the teams take a halftime break. Following halftime, the teams switch sides on the court. If, at the end of the fourth quarter, the score is tied, the game will run into overtime play, which lasts until the tie is broken by the end of a set amount of time.

Dribbling Around

When a team is in possession of the ball they are playing offensively. As I mentioned before, the objective of these players is to move the ball down-court and toss the ball into the other team's basket.

There are two ways to move the ball down-court: passing and dribbling. Passing sounds simple enough, but keep in mind that the other team is going to be trying to prevent you from tossing the ball to your teammates. They may even try to strip the ball out of your hands and steal it for themselves. What may seem a simple lob to a teammate can turn into a complicated task when everybody else on the court is presenting either a moving target (your teammates) or a possible interception (the opposing players).

If you don't have the ball in your hands, you are pretty much free to move about the court, with only a few restrictions. However, once you get the ball, your movement becomes highly restricted. If you want to move about with the ball, you are required to dribble.

Dribbling is an odd sort of dance where you must bounce the ball between your hand and the floor repeatedly as you move about the court. You may never take more than one and a half steps between ball bounces. If you do, you will incur a penalty called travelling and the ball will be given to the opposing team.

Your objective while you dribble is to maneuver yourself – and let your teammates maneuver themselves – into position so you can either take a shot at the basket, or pass the ball to another player.

Dribbling is an art in itself. Skilled dribblers can outmaneuver their opponents with a combination of well-timed footwork and body language that fakes out the other team. Even though you are not allowed to touch the ball with both hands while dribbling, you *can* bounce the ball from one hand to the other to allow you to quickly change direction or get the ball away from opponents who are in a position to steal the ball.

If you hold the ball in both hands or stop dribbling, you are allowed to only move one foot. The other foot remains anchored to the floor, providing a pivot point so you can move your free leg around to find an advantageous angle from which to either hand the ball off to another player or take a shot at the basket.

If you start dribbling again after you have stopped, this activity is known as double dribbling. The penalty for double dribbling: you lose possession of the ball.

The Rest of the Team

If a teammate has the ball, you aren't just standing around, watching. While we'll discuss specific player positions and responsibilities in a moment, here are a few things you'll have on your mind:

- You want to position yourself so that you are free to receive the ball. Of course, this will be complicated by the fact that the other team's players will try to get between you and the ball, so you'll have to keep moving around them into the open.

- If you're in the key, you *really* want to keep on the move! The key is the area under the basket and in front of it. This area is clearly marked on the floor, and you can only be inside it for three seconds at a time. Consequently, you and your teammates may be constantly churning in and out of this area, all the while evading defensive players and trying to keep free to receive the ball for a quick layup. I told you this is a dynamic game!

- If you're not doing the dizzy dance in and out of the key, you still have the fun of positioning yourself so you can receive the ball and either dribble, pass to another player, or shoot it into the basket. The fun includes eluding your opponents, whose job it is to keep you from getting easy access to the ball.

- At the same time you have to be totally aware...of everything!
    - The shot clock – In professional play your team has 24 seconds to attempt a shot. Playing strategies may change if the clock is about to expire.
    - Where your teammates are located, at the moment.
    - Where your opponents are located, at the moment
    - Where your blocker is headed (so you can go the other way!)

When a team is not in possession of the ball it is playing defense.

- The objective of the defense is to prevent the offense from earning points by sinking a basket.
- Defensive players accomplish this by impeding a player from making progress down the court, by blocking the person with the ball to prevent him from passing it off to another player, by blocking players that hope to receive a pass, or by stealing the ball outright from the offense.

Players and Positions

Center – The center is positioned near the basket and is often a tall player. On offense, the role of the center is to get open so a teammate can pass the ball to her for an easy point shot. If she cannot get open, her secondary job is to block defenders to free up other players on the team. Defensively, the center's role is to block shots and passes inside the key and to catch rebounds.

Forward – Forwards play in the wing and corner areas as well as right under the basket. Forwards are usually the second tallest players. On the offense, the role of the forward is to get open so other players can pass the ball to him. Forwards also take outside shots. On the defense, the role of the forward is to prevent rebounds and interrupt drives to the goal.

Guard – Guards are usually the third tallest players on a team. They are responsible for moving the ball down the court and executing offensive plays. Guards must be good at dribbling, analyzing the court, and passing to other players. They must also be able to shoot from the perimeter of the court. The defensive objective of the guard is to steal passes, prevent drives to the goal, and to contest shots.

Equipment and Gear

First, you need a **basketball** to play with. Most sporting goods and department stores sell basketballs. You can buy one that is traditionally orange or select from any number of colors and designs. Competitive basketball requires a ball with characteristics as follows: The WNBA requires a ball that weighs 20 ounces and has a circumference of 29 inches. The NBA ball weighs in at 22 ounces with a circumference of 30 inches. Both balls must be an approved shade of orange with a pebbled or composite cover.

If you have a basketball, you can turn almost anything into a **basketball court**. There are many ways to find or make a court. You can turn your driveway or a small portion of a street into a small half-court. You can also find basketball courts in parks or recreation areas. Finally, many basketball games are played in a gym.

Unique to basketball is the **hoop** and **backboard**. Many will be permanently fixed wherever there is a court to play on. However, without much difficulty, you can purchase your own hoop on a pole with a base to support it that can be moved to the side of a driveway or the curb of a street.

On both ends of the basketball court is the **hoop**. The hoop is eighteen inches in diameter, an orange medal ring with fasteners for a mesh net. The hoop must be at least ten feet above the court and is affixed to the **backboard**. The backboard is a 6 by 3.5 foot piece of material that the ball bounces off when a player makes a shot. The backboard is centered between the sidelines and positioned four feet in from the baseline.

A standard basketball court boasts a shiny, hard, wooden floor and is built in the shape of a rectangle. The actual dimensions of the court depend on the level of ball being played. A professional NBA, NCAA or WNBA court is 94 by 50 feet, while the typical high school court should be 84 by 50 feet. The size is reduced to 74 by 42 feet for middle school.

A set of lines on any standard court marks the different sections:

The **baselines** signify where the bounds of the court are on each end. If a player has the ball and steps on or outside these lines, the other team gets the ball.

The **sidelines** mark the boundary for play on the sides of the court. The ball is considered out of bounds if you are holding it and step on or outside these lines.

The **half court line** runs straight across the middle of the court between the sidelines, dividing it into two equal halves.

The **free throw line** is fifteen feet in from the baseline. If a player fouls another player who is attempting to shoot a basket, he may be allocated from one to three free-throw shots from this line.

The **three-point line** is an arc that divides the two-point and three-point scoring sections. If a player nails a shot from behind this line, the team is awarded three points. If a player is fouled while taking a shot from behind this line, he is given three foul shots.

The **key** is a keyhole-shaped area beneath the basket with rules that prevent players from lingering there. It also defines the area behind which both teams wait while foul shots are taken.

The **center circle** is (you guessed it) a circle in the very center of the court where two players face off for the beginning jump-shot. At the start of a game, the referee tosses the ball into the air and two players, one from each team, jump straight up and try to tip the ball toward a waiting teammate.

Most professional courts have an electronic **scoreboard** to show how much time is left in a quarter and to display the current points for each team.

In terms of gear, you will need a **basketball uniform** to play a competitive game. A typical uniform consists of a jersey, made of moisture-wicking material with the player's number and last name on the back. The jersey represents the team by featuring the team's colors. You'll also need a pair of shorts and a pair of high-top athletic shoes, preferably with socks. The shorts must fall to one inch above the player's knee. College teams are allowed to wear a t-shirt underneath their jersey but NBA teams cannot. Optionally, you can choose to wear accessories such as **headbands, wristbands** or **armbands.** Slick Watts and Bill Walton started this trend in the 1970's. Many players wear these accessories to absorb body sweat, or to provide support and protection.

Another popular accessory is a **water bottle** to ensure adequate hydration. It is highly recommended that you carry a water bottle with you to practices, games and workout sessions. Many big box stores such as Wal-Mart, the Sports Authority and Dick's Sporting Goods offer a wide variety of water bottles, as well as online retailers.

Chapter 2: Stretching and Warm-Up Techniques

Stretching and warming up play an important part in your preparation for both practice and competition. By doing this regularly, you can increase your body's flexibility and decrease your chances of incurring a serious injury. To get warmed up, start out by moving around to gradually elevate your heart rate and get your blood circulating. Walking, jogging in place, or a few jumping jacks will serve this purpose. Then, begin to stretch each of the muscle groups in your body. You may wish to use some of the following stretches:

Split Stance Spine Rotation – This stretch targets your spine and can help you quickly change directions. Begin in a split stance with your right leg forward and your hands behind your head. Slowly rotate your upper body to the right and then return to center. Then rotate to the left and return to center. Repeat this stretch ten times.

Hamstring Stretch – This stretch targets your hamstring muscles, located in the back of your leg. Sit on the floor with your legs straight ahead of you. Roll your left leg outward and bend your knee, sliding the bottom of your left foot up the inside of your right leg until your foot rests against the upper inner thigh. Keeping your back straight, lean forward until you feel a stretch in the back of your right leg. Hold for twenty to thirty seconds and then return slowly to the starting position. Repeat this process to stretch the left leg

Standing Side Lean Quad Stretch – This stretch targets your quadriceps. Stand tall, then step forward with your left leg. Stretch your arms straight up. Tip the bottom of your hips forward then stretch your arms, leaning your upper body to the left. Straighten up and step back to return to your original position. Repeat this process, stepping forward with your right leg and stretching your torso to the right side.

Split Stance Spine Rotation – Begin in a split stance, with your right leg forward. With your hands behind your head, twist your upper body to the right and then return to face forward. Repeat this motion ten times, and then reverse your stance, placing your left foot forward and rotating to the left.

Back Stretch – This stretch targets your back muscles. Lie on the floor with your knees bent and your feet flat on the floor. Grasping your right leg below the knee, slowly pull it toward your chest, keeping your head on the ground. Hold your leg for thirty seconds, then slowly return to the starting position. Repeat with the left leg. Perform this stretch three times for each leg. Finally, use your arms to pull both legs toward your chest. Hold this position for thirty seconds, giving your back muscles an opportunity to relax before straightening your legs.

Rotating Stomach Stretch – This stretch targets your abdominal muscles and your lower back. Lie on your stomach with your hands at your shoulders. Look straight ahead and push with your arms to raise your upper body off the floor, keeping your hips and lower body on the ground. Look to the left as you gently bend your right arm so as to rotate your right shoulder toward the ground and stretch your torso toward the left. Hold for ten seconds, and then return to the centered stance. Repeat the stretch to the right, holding for ten seconds, then returning to center. Lower your torso to the starting position.

Wall Lat Stretch – This stretch targets back muscles that can help improve your jumping and defensive moves. Position yourself facing a wall, but two feet back. Lean forward, bending at the hips until your back is parallel to the floor. Placing your hands against the wall, allow them to stretch slightly backward. Hold for twenty seconds, and then return to the original position.

Groin Butterfly Stretch – This stretch targets the muscles in your groin area. Begin by sitting on the floor with your legs straight forward. Pull your legs toward you and place the soles of your feet together. Hold your feet together with your hands and pull your feet back toward the groin area. Rest your elbows on your thighs and gently press your legs down toward the floor. Hold for twenty seconds and then return slowing to the starting position.

Quad Stretch – This stretch isolates your quadriceps muscles much more effectively than that standing quad stretch. Lie on your left side, with your left leg bent in front of you. Bending your right leg back toward your hips, grasp your right foot with your right hand and gently pull, maintaining this stretch for about twenty seconds before releasing. Roll over onto your right side and repeat the process of stretching your left leg. Remember to always bend the bottom knee up to about waist height; this is key to isolating the quad muscles and avoiding engagement with your lower spine.

Single Heel Drop Achilles Stretch – Step onto a raised object, such as a small stepstool or one step on a flight of stairs. With your hand touching a wall or other stable object, rest the ball of your right foot on the edge. Let your knee bend slightly and slowly allow your heel to drop down until you feel the stretch in the back of your ankle. Hold this stretch for ten seconds, then slowly raise back up to the starting position and release. Repeat the process with the left foot.

Shoulder Stretch – This stretch targets your shoulder muscles. Stand with your feet about shoulder width apart. Move your right arm forward, placing your hand on your left shoulder. Put your left hand on your right elbow and pull it toward your right shoulder until you feel the stretch in your right shoulder. Hold for twenty seconds and release. Then, repeat with the left arm, stretching the left shoulder.

Hamstring Rocker – This stretch targets your hamstrings and improves hip mobility. Begin by standing upright, then step forward with your right foot to create a split stance. Bend over and rest your hands on the ground on either side of your right leg. Bend your right knee, lowering your hips, then straighten your right leg to bring your hips back up. Repeat this motion ten times, then return to the starting position. Perform the same motion with the left foot forward.

Arm Stretch – This exercise loosens your arms muscles and warms them up, readying them for action. Stand with your arms extended out from your sides. Begin by moving them in small circular motions and gradually make the circles larger until your arms are circling vertically; then reduce the circles until you have returned to the starting position. Repeat this motion, circling in the opposite direction.

Chapter 3: Improving Your Game

Practice Passing Strategies

Passing skills are important because in a game you will pass the ball until a player can find an open shot. While you can find all sorts of complicated passes on the internet, there are two basic types of shots in basketball: the **chest pass** and the **bounce pass**.

The chest pass consists of passing the ball to a teammate by pushing the ball straight out from your chest. The ball does not bounce or arch. The chest pass is the fastest and easiest way to pass the ball. The bounce pass occurs when you pass the ball from either your chest or waist but it bounces once before reaching your teammate's hands. It is hard for defenders to block bounce passes because the ball remains low to the ground.

To make effective passes, there are a few things to keep in mind:

1. Always use both hands to pass the ball. This enables you to better control it and allows you to give the ball a backspin.

2. Always put weight into your pass so the ball has proper velocity. If you can, step forward as you pass.

3. Make your pass effective by determining the speed at which you need to pass the ball and by reading the body language of your teammates. If a teammate is open and nearby, you don't need to chuck the ball hard. The farther you are from your teammate, the harder you will need to pass the ball, to avoid it being intercepted by an opponent.

4. Avoid tipped passes by passing the ball to the side of your teammate that is away from the defender. Try passing to your teammate's off side, away from the direction the defender is leaning or moving.

5. Don't over-think your pass. Newer players often try complicated passes, thinking they are more likely to trick their defenders, but that strategy is risky. Stick to passes that are straightforward and that make sense. Otherwise, you risk losing the ball to the other team.

6. Watch where the hands of your teammates are located. When your teammate has his hands near his shooting pocket, it means he is getting ready for a shot. If your teammate has his hands up, throw the ball toward his fingertips.

7. Avoid jumping while passing. If you jump and land while still in possession of the ball, it is considered a travelling offense.

8. When passing, make sure you know to whom you're passing. If you just throw the ball in the general vicinity of several teammates, you may have just handed it off to the other team.

9. Always use both hands to catch the ball. Use your muscles to control the ball in case it's in an awkward spin.

10. When the ball is passed to you, move toward the ball to catch it; this minimizes the chances of an interception.

You can use these drills to build your passing strength:

Overhead Pass Drill – Stand three feet from another player and face each other. Begin by holding the ball overhead, keeping your elbows straight. Keep your hands curved on the ball, with only your fingertips touching the surface. Flex your wrists back as far as possible and flick them forward without letting go of the ball. Flick your wrists again but this time release the ball to your partner. Do not use your arms for the release. You and the other player should spend five minutes flicking the ball back and forth, changing pivot feet each time.

Rapid Fire Passing Drill – All players line up two feet in front of a wall. Everyone should begin to rapid-fire passes against the wall, taking two steps back with each pass, until they are standing ten feet away. Then they should begin moving toward the wall again until they are back where they started. Each player should make twenty passes in all.

Proper Passing Drill – Start this drill by holding your arms over your head. Keep your elbows straight, your palms facing forward and your fingers spread apart. Stat flicking your your wrists back and then let them flex forward. Keeping your elbows straight, gently move your arms to the right. Bend your knees as you move your arms down, while continuing to flick your wrists. Bring your arms back over your head and then move them to the left, bending your knees again. Repeat this drill four times.

Triangle Passing Drill – Your team should divide into two groups. Designate three passing lines at each basket, making sure they are separated by fifteen feet. Place one line near the key, one in the right short corner and one in the left short corner. The ball should start near the key and players should pass in either direction. Once the pass is made, players should sprint to the next line. Players should switch up the types of passes they make throughout this drill.

Pivot Passing Drill – Stand three feet from another player. Begin by holding the ball overhead. Keeping your elbows straight, bend your wrists back as far as you can. Pass the ball to the other player by flicking your wrists. The other player must catch the ball and assign their left foot as the pivot. Before passing the ball back, that player must pivot around one time. The next time she catches the ball, the right foot should be used as the pivot.

One player will be the passer and the other will be the receiver. The receiver should start communicating with the passer where to throw the ball. Start by using hand signals. After five minutes, the receiver should change the method of communication. Players can use any type of body language, such as eye, head or hand movements. Change communication methods every two minutes.

Circle Pass Drill – Players form a large circle in the middle of the court. One player stands in the center of the circle. The first player with the ball passes it to the center of the circle and follows the ball to the center of the circle. The player in the center will pass the caught ball to the next player in the circle and run out to take the place of the first player. The player who receives the ball should pass it back to the player in the circle and then run in to switch places with the player in the center.

Swap or Pass Drill – Players should break into pairs and pass the ball between them. One player will throw a chest pass and the other, a bounce pass. The coach or another player will say "swap," to tell players to switch their type of pass. This drill helps players build timing and catching skills.

Practice Your Shooting Skills

Perfecting your shooting skills is important because successful shots are what will help bring your team to victory. However, shooting is a skill that requires frequent practice; you don't become an ace shooter overnight.

While shooting is a physical skill, a large part of it is mental. Mental discipline is essential to practice at the same time that you practice physically. Be patient with yourself. Remind yourself that you will have to miss some shots before you can start to sink them consistently. Remember that you're only human and nobody can make every shot one hundred percent of the time. Do not let the circumstances of the game distract you – your coach will handle that; just focus on playing the game.

A good way to increase your shot percentage is to figure out what kinds of shots you are best at. Practice a couple sets of layups, open shots, jump shots, post shots and slam dunks and measure them in terms of what comes easiest for you and which shots you have the most success with. To get good at these shots, you can practice this basic shooting form that helps with most shots:

Square your shoulders to the hoop. With your shooting hand, position your fingers under the ball and keep your elbows close to your body. Use your non-shooting hand to gently balance the ball. Aim the ball toward the middle of the rim. Bring your shooting arm up to the basket and release the ball by flicking your wrist. The power of your wrist flick and the force of your fingers are what will guide the ball into the basket. You can use this basic form to master:

Layups – A layup is considered the most basic shot in basketball. It is executed by a player who is near the hoop. In a layup, you use one hand to throw the ball toward the backboard as you jump toward the basket.

Jump Shots – The jump shot is used for mid to long range shots. At short range, you can use it to escape a defender by outjumping him. Using the basic shooting form, jump straight up and release the ball at the top of your jump.

Free Throws – The free throw utilizes the basic shooting form from a flat-footed standing start.

Slam Dunks – Slam dunks are a signature shot of basketball and generally rely on your ability to jump rather than shoot. If you can jump high enough, you will put the ball above the rim and force it through the basket.

Three-point Shots – It also takes practice to master the three-point shot. Three-pointers are tricky because once a player steps behind the three-point line, his form tends to shift. The best way to master this shot is to simply practice shooting, but in different phases. Start by standing ten feet from the basket. Practice shots from this point until it feels natural. Then take a step back and practice more shots until this location feels natural. Keep doing this until you are comfortable with taking a shot from behind the three-point line While you will be shooting thousands of baskets before you reach three-point distance, you will also be improving your ability to make two-point shots from a variety of closer spots on the court.

The best strategy for perfecting your shots is to enlist a coach or an experienced player to mentor you. Stick with a single person for shooting advice. Everybody has a different approach, so if you listen to more than one person, all the conflicting advice may actually make your shooting worse.

Foul Shots – The last type of shot you should be able to master is the foul shot. You never know – you could be making a foul shot with five seconds left in the game and your team might need that one point to tie the game! All foul shots are set up the same – you stand fifteen feet straight back from the rim.

Successful foul shots are half form, half psychology. You should create a specific form and stick with it. Foul shots are easily practiced by yourself. Before releasing the ball, take time to focus your energies and think positive affirmations such as, "I will easily make this shot and bring my team to victory." If negative thoughts pop up such as, "If I miss this basket my team will lose," your chances of making the shot may be dramatically reduced. Wipe them out of your mind by repeating positive affirmations.

Practice Your Dribble

Mastering your dribbling ability requires a combination of practice and skill development. The best strategy is to build up to the hardest dribbling drills you can find and keep working at them until they feel comfortable. Choose drills that will enable you to practice with either hand. If you wish, you can practice them while standing in place until you get comfortable, but it is most effective when you practice dribbling while moving up and down the court. Mastering dribbling drills can outfit you with confidence in a number of situations you'll face on the court.

Players often feel a great deal of pressure when dribbling the ball downcourt on a fresh possession. Your main objective is to get the ball to the defensive half of the court so your team can execute a play, but the pressure can cause players to linger excessively in the middle of the court with the ball. Practice your dribbling until you feel confident while handling the ball. This will protect you from any pressure to turn your back or change your rhythm, which can allow the other team to steal the ball.

Here are some dribbling drills you can use to build up your confidence:

Pound Dribbles – Dribble the ball in front of you so that it bounces up to your waist. Slowly begin to bounce the ball harder until you can dribble it as high as possible without jumping. Slowly dribble the ball softer until you can get on one knee and dribble it. Then pound the ball to keep it bouncing and repeat the drill with your other hand.

Power Crossovers – Intensely dribble the ball with one hand and then quickly bounce it to your other hand. Repeat this exercise, starting with the alternate hand.

Kill Dribbles – Bounce the ball until it bounces up to your waist and then quickly "kill" it by dribbling it extremely low to the ground. Bring it back up and repeat this drill a few times with both hands.

Blind Dribble – Put a blindfold over your eyes or close them. Dribble intensely for about one minute. To enhance this drill, start moving around as you dribble. To add even more challenge, intensely dribble two balls at once as you move around.

Circle Dribbles – Step your left leg forward and dribble the ball around it in a circle. Repeat for your right leg. After going around both legs, try to dribble the ball around both legs in the shape of a figure eight.

10-5 Dribbles – Choose one hand to practice with. Dribble intensely for ten seconds and then slow to a gentle dribble for five seconds. Repeat until your hand has gotten a good workout. This drill helps train you to alternate dribble speeds on the court.

Dribbling Between Legs – Intensely dribble as you walk up and down the court. As you move, practice dribbling the ball between your legs. To enhance this drill try walking at a quicker pace or transitioning to a light trot.

Lying Down Double Drill – Lie on your back and dribble the ball. Count out ten seconds, sit up and dribble the ball under your legs to your other hand. Lie back down and repeat the process, dribbling constantly the whole time.

Double Ball Dribbling – Intensely dribble a ball in each hand at the same time. This drill helps build arm strength and dribble control. It also helps you learn how to dribble without looking at the ball.

Dribbling Sprints – Stand at a baseline. Intensely dribble and sprint to the foul line and back. Dribble to the middle of the court and go back. Dribble again to the farthest foul line and go back. Finally, dribble and sprint the full length of the court. This drill helps you build direction-changing abilities as well as your speed and dribble ability. You can choose to do one cycle of this drill or repeat it as needed.

Three-Cone Dribbles – Spread out three cones in a line with ten feet in between each one. Intensely dribble around each cone in different shapes, such as a square, a triangle, or a figure eight. This drill allows you to use a little imagination while working on your speed and movement.

Dirt Dribbling – Find a patch of dirt and intensely dribble on it for two minutes. Since dirt is a softer surface than a court, this drill will force you to dribble harder, thus giving your arms a good workout.

Synergize Your Skills

Effective basketball players don't limit themselves to certain strengths while letting weaknesses slide; they try to synergize their skills to become the best overall players possible. While not every player can have equally balanced strengths, it is important to master each of the basic skills of passing, catching, shooting, dribbling, ball-handling, and footwork. The more you focus on developing each of these skills, the more your skills will blend together smoothly into an effective whole. This is because each skill builds off the other. The better you are at passing, the better you will get at catching. The better you are at dribbling, the better you will be at making shots.

Have a Plan for Every Practice

Before you begin a practice time, plan out what you're going to work on and decide how long you'll spend practicing. When you practice you have the option of working on your weaknesses and building up your strengths. It's advisable to work on both strengths and weakness in each practice session, but to focus on a different skill each time. You can practice shooting and dribbling first, to get them out of the way and warm up at the same time.

Find the courage to push yourself out of your comfort zone when practicing. This is the time to take risks, experiment, and find out what you can make work for you. Have some goofy fun while you work, too. Don't worry about messing up or looking stupid. When you practice at home you won't be working in front of an audience (unless you include any nosy neighbors).

Put Ultimate Effort and Focus into Your Practice

Putting maximum and ultimate effort and focus into your practices can help push you closer to your ideal as a player. People who are passionate about basketball will find this easy (at least most of the time).

If you don't have a passion for basketball, or at least enjoy the game, this may not be the right sport for you. You can usually tell if an employee doesn't like her job because she doesn't contribute enthusiastically. Sports are no different. If you enjoy the challenge, your attitude is in the right place, and you give it your all every time, you will find yourself on an expedited track to near-perfection.

Repetition is Key to Skill Development

Repetition is what will help you become an ultimate basketball star. However, it's important that you practice correct technique. Remember this important tip: only perfect repetition leads to perfect execution. Keep working on drills until they become natural for you. When you've perfected drills through repetition, your chances of perfect execution in the middle of a game are much higher.

Simulate Real-game Scenarios During Practice

Practicing for perfect execution is important to flexibility in a highly dynamic competitive environment, but simulating real-life conditions during practice can up your preparedness dramatically. The key to simulating a game scenario is to repeatedly practice things that commonly happen in every game. Some of these scenarios include:

- Returning to Defense

    When you are playing offense, ensure that your team fully converts to defense after the shot. Have your coach or another player blow a whistle or yell a command to signify that your team has fully returned to defense.

- Passing/Catching on Offense

To work on your passing and catching while on offense, try this drill: Put fifteen balls on a rack and remove one for every bad pass or interception. Once all the balls have been removed, players must run a sprint for every bad pass or turnover for the rest of the practice.

- Adjusting defense to match offensive moves

    Play at least two timed minutes of defense for each practice. If all players don't perfectly adjust to the offensive players, the clock starts over and the drill doesn't end until the defense plays perfectly.

- Shooting

    See the section on shooting to work on perfecting this skill.

- Rebounds

    Rebounds should be the last thing you work on, both offensively and defensively. During every practice, at least three players on the offense should crash on each shot while the defense attempts to block every rebound.

Practice in Different Groups

One of the great things about basketball is that you can break down into different sized groups, both for practice and for fun play. Depending on your group size, you can focus on strengthen specific skills. Here are some of the potential group sizes and how to optimize your work within them:

Practice by Yourself – Practicing by yourself is the best way to develop your individual skills and build up your weaknesses. Maximize this opportunity to focus on shooting or dribbling as opposed to passing and catching, which require at least two people to accomplish.

One-on-One – Practicing one on one can help you learn to defend single players. This is also a good way to focus on your shooting when another body is in your way.

Three-on-Three – Practicing three-on-three provides a simulation of a full court game. Street ball is often played three-on-three. This configuration allows you to work on team strategies as well as honing personal skills.

Five-on-Five – This configuration mirrors the structure of a real game and is always played on a full court. It provides the full benefits of focus on both team and personal skills. Five-on-five ball builds stamina since there are no substitutions in this scenario. You will be running back and forth on the court and active the entire time.

Don't Let Your Size Define You

It is true that size matters in basketball. Being tall is helpful when it comes making shots and successfully blocking offensive players. However, many shorter basketball players have been highly successful. The key to utilizing your size in basketball is to figure out your strengths and weaknesses and make the most of your strengths. For example, you may not be all that great at making slam dunks if you lack maximum stature, but you might be highly successful at layup shots. You may find it difficult to block tall offensive players but your speed and agility may help your team quickly maneuver the ball around taller – and sometimes slower – players.

Learn to Apply Drillwork in Games

When performing drills, it is important to think how these actions would be used when playing a real game. Ask yourself important questions like, "Where is the defense located?" or "Where are my teammates on the court?" Use stationary objects such as cones or chairs to build a mock scenario that allows you to practice a variety of situations.

Find a Mentor and Keep Open to Coaching

One of the best ways to improve as a basketball player is to find a mentor and keep yourself open to coaching. Many players are hesitant to embrace coaching because it involves criticism. That's natural; nobody likes to be criticized. However, criticism can help you take great strides forward in your playing, if you don't let it get the best of you.

The key is to choose to trust a person to speak truth into your life. Even if it hurts. In the past, you have probably been exposed to criticism that was *not* given with your best interests in mind. However, if you value knowing the truth about your playing, you must put yourself in a place where you can take in all criticism, even words that are not all that kind, and milk those words for anything good you can gain from them. If you can do this, *then* you are in a place where you can begin to make genuine progress.

Here's a tip: don't wait for a mentor to come to you. Seek one out yourself. Your mentor can be anybody who is willing to share valuable information that will help you grow, such as a coach, a more experienced player, a personal trainer, or even a nutritionist.

Use Technology to Your Advantage

There are many different ways to learn; in basketball, video training is one of the best. There are two types of videos you will find useful: taping actual games and instructional videos. While it's common to review your own games, and this can be highly informative, you can also learn from replaying professional games.

By taping a professional game, you can learn straight from the pros. You can watch a game over and over again, replaying events to study what the players do individually and as a team. You can review how they react in different situations and begin to train your instantaneous responses, even extending these strategies to practice drills. Tape and review as many games as you can; some people I know have up to 300 games recorded!

Instructional videos also come in handy. With the popularity of online video sites like YouTube, training is easy to access. Instructional videos help you self-coach. You can use them to take yourself from average player status to being a really great one!

Here are some helpful YouTube instructional YouTube videos for starters:

- Basketball Training Kobe Bryant ALL-IN-ONE by eBA Basketball Channel A

- Basketball shooting tips and drills. Form shooting with Rob McClanaghan by ProTips4U

- Michael Jordan's Basketball Lesson by theshot2

If you want to take this tactic the extra mile, film yourself as you practice. This will allow you to view yourself from a third-person perspective and will help you identify your strengths and weaknesses. This is especially useful when working on your shooting skills; use it to pinpoint strengths and weaknesses in your form.

Recognize Both Your Strengths and Your Weaknesses

Based on the demands of your role on the court, make a list of your strengths and weaknesses. Be honest in your assessment.

First look at your list of weaknesses. What drills can you implement to help you strengthen these areas?. Consider videotaping yourself to gain another perspective. Ask yourself:

- Do I understand this skill and what it takes to master it?

- Is this weakness due to a lack of physical strength?

- Is it an issue of flexibility or coordination?

- What is my mental <u>attitude</u> when I approach this performance weakness?

Your answers to these questions can help you determine where to focus your attention. In addition to designing exercises to appropriately target these areas of weakness, I advise you to research how others have addressed this particular issue. I'll bet you can find a few training videos out there that can help, since your weakness is anything but unique. Your teammates – and your opponents – are probably already aware of your weaknesses, and may be willing to provide advice on how to counter them effectively. Their advice may be well worth the price, even if it does mean eating a massive helping of humble pie in the process.

While it is important to accept your abilities – both strengths and weaknesses – as part of being human, most weaknesses can be improved with proper training, if not completely eradicated. The challenge is for you to learn to employ your portfolio of abilities so that you are working effectively with all of them, not fighting some while reveling in others.

Even your weaknesses have their place. They can be useful in specific situations. Concentrate on finding a few ways where each specific weakness can be used to your advantage on the court. Your primary task is to learn how to blend all of your abilities into a whole person who responds effectively to every situation.

Don't Neglect Your Strengths

Don't neglect your strengths in favor of strengthening your weaknesses. In light of your weaknesses, it's easy to think you can let your strengths slide. While it's good to be a well-balanced player, it's actually counterproductive to create balance by "dumbing down" your strengths to a level compatible with your weaknesses! What you want to do is sustain and even increase your strengths, so they can continue to carry you and your team forward, while you work to sharpen the areas in which you are weak. Monitor your personal practice times to include work on both strengths and weaknesses.

Chapter 4: Basketball Strength Training

Basketball requires the use of a mixture of muscles. Most players have to run, pivot and jump, which uses the muscles in your feet and legs. Jumping is one of the most important moves in basketball and requires you to have strong ab muscles, calf muscles, hamstrings, quadriceps, and glutes. When you develop a strength training routine, it is important to equally target all these muscles, as well as your core for stability. Players should not begin to strength train until they are in their late teens, as the body goes through several changes before that time, including the continued development of muscle tissue.

To properly train as a basketball player, there are three primary components to develop: **explosiveness**, **strength**, and **endurance**. To increase explosiveness, the key is to perform as many repetitions of an exercise as you can within twenty seconds. Don't exceed twenty seconds or you will actually be training your body to move slower. Complete three sets of repetitions for each exercise, resting for five minutes between each set.

To develop strength, you want to perform six to twelve repetitions of an exercise in three sets, with three minutes of rest between each. If you are using weights, you will increase them as your strength increases.

To develop endurance, perform an exercise 25 times in two sets with a ninety-second rest period in between. Use lighter weights to build endurance, making it easy to perform the higher number of reps.

- Always train using correct form and stop when you feel your form slipping. Some athletes make the mistake of continuing to train with poor form just to get in a few extra sets. However, training with bad form can ultimately lead to bad performance or injury.

- Always ensure that you're training with basketball-specific exercises. Focusing on the wrong muscle groups will not help you when you're out on the court. It is important to start out with less weight and fewer repetitions if you're a beginner. You can always work your way up. Putting too much strain on untrained muscles can result in ligament injuries.

When you design your personal workouts, you have the ability to be flexible and creative. One of the most popular options is to do a full body workout two to three times a week with a different focus each session. Here is one way to divide up your practices:

- Tuesday: Explosiveness

- Thursday: Strength
- Saturday: Endurance

The next most popular option is to work out four to six times a week, alternating between working your upper and your lower body. For example:

- Monday: Explosiveness (upper body)
- Wednesday: Strength (lower body)
- Friday: Endurance (upper body)
- Saturday: Explosiveness (lower body)

Depending on the current part of the playing season, the focus of your workout will vary. It is common for athletes to focus on building strength and explosiveness after the playing season has ended. As the next performance time approaches, the emphasis shifts toward endurance training. Alternatively, you can work on all three areas in the same week. However, not all athletes are the same, so customize your workout routine to meet your specific requirements.

Everybody has a different mix of physical strengths and weaknesses; while one athlete may need equal focus on all three characteristics, another may only need to emphasize one aspect. When you plan your routine, ask yourself what you need to improve the most. If you happen to already be well-balanced, then create a workout that is well-balanced. If you're new to working out, it is best to focus on one area at a time and then move on to another.

During the preseason, it is important work out at least two times a week. Once the season is over, you should allow your body to rest for a while. Recovery time is just as important as the time you spend building muscles. After allowing time for your muscles to heal, begin implementing a strategic mix of strength training exercises to build up your explosiveness, endurance, and strength for the next season.

Explosive Exercises

Plate Jump

This exercise enables you to jump hard and fast. Stand straight while holding a twenty-pound plate in both hands. Pull the plate to your chest as you crouch with your legs. Then push the plate up and out with as much force as possible while you jump straight up. As you come back down into a crouching position, pull the plate back toward your chest. The force of the plate will assist in pulling you up, even higher than would be normal otherwise. It will also force you to go with the plate in order to keep your balance. Perform this exercise in three sets of eight jumps.

Bench Lateral Jump

This exercise targets your legs. Position yourself to the left of a bench. Jump onto the bench as hard as you can with both feet. Jump down to the right. Jump back up using the same method you used in the beginning and then jump down to the left side. Perform this exercise in three sets of ten repetitions.

Squatting Frog Jump

The squatting frog jump lets you practice switching from slow to fast muscle contractions. Stand straight and hold a dumbbell vertically in your hands. Keeping your lower back flat, squat down until the dumbbell touches the ground in between your feet. At this point perform the most powerful vertical jump you can. Do not bend your arms. Perform this exercise in three sets of eight jumps.

Single Leg Lateral Bench Jumps

This exercise targets your legs. Stand next to a bench and balance yourself on your right leg. Jump using your right leg as powerfully as you can onto the bench. Jump down on the right side and then jump back using a powerful one-leg jump. Perform this exercise in three sets of ten repetitions for each leg.

Squatting Box Jump

Start by standing just in front of a box with a weight bar across the back of your neck and shoulders. Grasp the bar with an overhand grip, so that your elbows are pointing straight ahead. Keeping your heels against the box, tighten your lower back and sit on the box, as far back as possible. From there, perform the most powerful jump you possibly can.

Reverse Lunge Knee Up

Stand on one foot. Step back on your other foot so that you are standing in a reverse lunge position. Thrust your strength through your front foot and raise your opposite knee toward your chest. Step back. Repeat eight times, then switch feet and repeat the process.

Dumbbell Swing Jump

The dumbbell swing jump targets your hips. Stand with your feet wider apart than your shoulders, holding one end of a dumbbell in your arms, allowing them to hang and relax. Forcefully swing the dumbbell back between your legs. You can allow your head to drop so that you can reach back further. Ignoring the weight, push your hips forward and jump. When your hips extend, the dumbbell will swing faster. When the weight swings upward, it will pull your body forward. This creates a strong force during the last phase of your jump. Perform this exercise for three sets of six jumps.

Plyo Push Up

Start out in the standard push-up position. Push your body up with enough power that you have time to clap your hands before they land back on the floor.

Lateral Jumps (a.k.a., Ski Hops)

Start on the left of center, with your weight on your left leg. Crouch down and explode up, leaping with all your force to the right and slightly forward. Catch yourself on the right foot, continuing into a crouch that explodes up and carries you back to the left side, where you land on your left leg. Repeat this until you have progressed forward about twenty feet.

Dumbbell Jerk

This exercise helps you practice getting down quickly. Align your shoulders and feet. Hold a dumbbell in each hand. Raise each one up to your shoulders, allowing them to rest on the edge of each shoulder. Crouch, then powerfully jump up as you extend your arms upward. Come down into a lunge position. Your arms should remain fully extended. Slowly bring yourself into a completely upright position. Perform this exercise in two sets of eight reps, alternating legs in the lunge.

Plyometric Deadlift

Stand on your left leg and, keeping your arms to your sides, bend over at your hips until your right leg is straight behind you and your chest is parallel to the ground. Quickly swing your arms forward, raise your chest up and jump, landing on your left leg. Slowly return to original position. Repeat, standing on your right leg.

Ravers

This exercise targets your calves and is good for stretching your muscles. Stand with a barbell across your shoulders. One foot should be forward and the other back. Slightly bend your knees and quickly jump up, reversing your before you come down. As you master this exercise, gradually begin to add weight to the barbell. Perform this exercise in three sets of fifteen jumps.

Concentric Box Jump

This exercise helps you build force from a static position. Position yourself in front of and facing a box. Start in a half squat. From that position, jump onto the box. Try to land in the middle and stand straight up. Perform this exercise for two sets of six repetitions.

Endurance Exercises

Full Court Basketball

Full court basketball in itself is a great endurance exercise, because you are constantly sprinting, jumping, and changing direction. The key to counting full court basketball as an endurance exercise is if you play at full speed. You cannot count a pick-up game as endurance training. The easiest way to remind yourself to play at full speed is to treat the practice like a real game.

Suicide Drills

Suicide drills are famous as a top endurance training exercise. Like full court basketball, they simulate live action games and force players to work on changing direction. Start by standing on one baseline and facing the other end of the court. Sprint to the free throw line, touch it and return to the baseline. Touch the baseline, sprint to the half court line and repeat. Repeat for the free throw line on the opposite end of the court, and then the far baseline. Once you have touched the opposite baseline, run through your starting baseline at full speed. When you have passed your starting baseline, you have completed one suicide.

Defensive Figure Eight

This exercise also simulates game motions but this one in particular uses lateral defense movements. Start at a baseline and line up along the right sideline. Sprint to the half court and then slide left to the left sideline. Next, sprint forward to the far baseline and slide to the right sideline. Back pedal to the half court line and slide across the half court line to the left sideline. Back pedal to your starting baseline and slide across it. The completed exercise should bring you around in a figure eight shape that covers the entire court.

Interval Training

Interval training combines sprinting and jogging in intervals. This type of exercise enables you to gain the benefits of running long distances without missing out on the good you get from sprinting. There are two ways to perform interval training, depending on your setting. If you are going to be training on a track, start out by sprinting for a certain amount of time or a certain distance and then rest your body by jogging for a predetermined time or distance before picking up your sprint again. If you're going to be doing this at home or in a gym, most machines have an interval cycle option where you can alternate with sprinting and jogging automatically.

Cardiovascular Activity

Any type of cardiovascular activity can count as endurance training. Cardio can help strengthen your heart and lungs because it increases your body's oxygen output. It also helps you burn calories and strengthens your large muscles while fending off a variety of diseases and ailments, including heart disease. There are many types of activities that count as cardio, including:

- **Swimming**

    Swimming is a great cardio exercise because it is fun and intensive swimming can burn as much as 350 calories in a half hour. Swimming just for fun can burn up to 250 calories in a half hour. If you spend a half hour swimming vigorously and a half hour swimming for fun, you can burn up to 600 calories in an hour. Swimming is a great way to keep your knees and heart strong.

- **Outdoor Biking**

    Bike riding is another fun way to get in some cardio work; it's also a great way to work out your lower body. Outdoor biking is more effective than stationary biking because it exposes you to variations in weather and terrain, giving you a better challenge. One great thing about biking is that you can go fast or slow; you can travel at your own pace. The amount of calories you burn while biking depends on your speed and the resistance of your terrain. In general, biking at ten miles per hour can burn as much as 372 calories over sixty minutes. If you ride at an average of twenty miles per hour, you can burn over 1,000 calories in one hour.

- **Jumping Rope**

    Jumping rope, even for a few minutes of your day, can do amazing things to your cardiovascular health. This simple workout can positively affect your whole body and as a plus, it helps improve your hand-eye-coordination. You can start out by jumping the traditional way, but for variety's sake, feel free to introduce alternate rope jumping techniques.

- **Jogging**

    Jogging is a step up from walking and can be performed outside or inside. Like biking, jogging outdoors is better because you can enjoy the fresh air as you traverse a variety of terrain. Start out slow and gradually increase your speed until you are jogging eight miles per hour, which is the optimum pace for burning calories.

- **Kickboxing**

Kickboxing is well-known as a source for cardiovascular exercise. It works out your entire body and strengthens your core muscles. Since you are constantly moving, it can also be a fun workout. You can do this at home or by taking a class, where you might be able to make new friends.

- **Body Combat**

    Body combat is a combination of boxing, karate, tai chi, taekwondo, and muay thai. This very energetic cardio workout consists of punching, striking, kicking, and performing other styles of martial arts while listening to music. Body combat can be a fun way to exercise because it is unlike other cardio exercises.

Yoga

Yoga is a type of exercise that promotes muscular endurance. It is a great way to strengthen your entire body and help it become more flexible. Anyone can do yoga, which makes it a great starting place for strength training. Since yoga can help restore your body, you can practice it on your off days between strength training sessions. Yoga can also strengthen your mind and soul, equipping you for the internal aspects of basketball.

One great yoga strength training position is the **dolphin plank**. To do this, lie down on your stomach and point your toes. With your forearms on the ground, pull your abdomen toward your back and raise your hips until you're in a straight planking position. While inhaling, lift your hips further until your body is in a V-shape. Hold this position for a few seconds before returning to your starting position. You can do this fifteen times in sets of three.

A second yoga position for strength training is the **curtsy lunge**. To do this, align your feet with your hips and then, while taking a big step back with your left foot, placing it on a line behind your right foot. Bend your left knee as you extend your left hand toward your right foot. For each side, you can repeat this exercise fifteen times in three sets.

A third yoga position for strength training is the **Superman** pose. To do this, lie on your stomach on the floor. Extend your arms and legs out from your body, then breathe in as you raise your arms and legs as high as possible. Hold this position for a few seconds before breathing out and slowly returning to your starting position. You can do this in three sets of fifteen.

A fourth yoga position for strength training is the **triangle.** for this exercise you will need a wooden block about one foot square. Place the block just behind your right foot. To perform this pose, stand with your legs wide apart. Turn your entire right leg out (or rotate the foot to the right) ninety degrees while turning your entire left leg in (or rotate your left foot to the right) fifteen degrees. Place your hands on your sides at your hips so you can feel their movement. While exhaling, bend to the right from where your hips meet your thighs (keeping your waist straight), and place your right hand on the block behind your right leg for stability. Raise your left arm up until it is vertical. Remain in this position, breathing slowly and deeply, for about thirty seconds. Slowly inhale and return your torso to its upright position and turn you feet to face forward again. Stand in this position for a few seconds before bringing your feet together.

Strength Training Exercises

Lunges

Lunges target your core muscles including your quadriceps, hamstrings, and hip flexors. They also help your body burn calories. You can perform a lunge with weights or just by using your own body weight.

Stand with your shoulders and feet aligned. Keep your head and toes facing straight ahead. Step your right foot forward and slowly lower your body. Make sure that your right knee does not extend forward past your toes. Lower yourself until your left thigh is aligned with the ground. You can let your left knee bend to help bring yourself lower but don't let it touch the ground. From here, you can either bring your right foot back and straighten yourself into your starting position, or you can use your left foot to step even with your right foot, then swing past your right foot and perform a lunge with the left leg forward.

Shrugs

This exercise targets your trapezius and shoulder muscles. Begin by standing with your feet and shoulders aligned. Position yourself in front of a barbell. Turn your palms inward and grasp the barbell with your hands, using a grip that is slightly wider than your shoulders. Raise the barbell until you're standing up completely. Exhale as you shrug your shoulders. Hold for a second and then inhale as you bring your shoulders back down. Repeat.

Squats

This exercise targets your quadriceps, calves, hamstrings, glutes, and core muscles. It is effective whether you use weights or just your body weight

Stand straight with your feet shoulder-width apart. Keep your toes pointed out at a thirty degree angle. Lower your body to the ground, keeping your back straight and your core muscles tight. Keep your hips back as you bend your knees. Lower yourself until your thighs are parallel with the ground. Slowly raise yourself back up, straightening your knees and hips until you're standing straight again. Repeat.

Ab Plate Twist

Ab plate twists target your abdominal muscles. To begin, sit on the floor with your legs extended. Hold a plate with two hands, like driving a car, and position it in front of your abs. Bend your knees slightly, cross your ankles, and gradually lift them up. Your back should remain straight but you can lean backwards a little to keep your body balanced. Exhale, twist your upper body to the right, and touch the plate to the ground. Inhale and return to your original position. Exhale, twist your upper body to the left, and touch the plate to the ground. Return to your original position. Repeat.

Pull Ups

Pull ups are an overall great exercise for your body. Pull ups mainly target your latissimus dorsi, the muscles that run from your armpit to your lower back. This muscle is commonly overlooked in other strength training exercises.

To begin, hold a pull-up bar with an overhand grip. Stick your chest out and squeeze your shoulder blades together so that your upper back arches slightly. Pull down to your shoulder blades, pulling your body up until your chin passes the bar. Repeat.

Barbell Row

This exercise targets your upper back, lower back, arms and hips. Begin by standing in front of a barbell. Bend down and grasp it with your hands, keeping your palms facing inward. Keep your upper body horizontal and pull the bar against your chest. Bring the bar back to the floor. Repeat.

Military Press

Military presses are great strength training exercises for basketball because they simulate ball handling in traffic. This exercise targets your deltoid, the central shoulder muscle.

Begin by sitting on a bench. Make sure your back is straight and your core muscles are stable. Hold a dumbbell in both hands and position them just above your shoulders. Press your arms upward until they are fully straight without locking your elbows. Slowly lower your arms. Repeat.

Dumbbell Press

This exercise targets your pectoral, triceps and deltoid muscles. Begin by lying down face-up on a bench with your feet planted flat on the floor. Hold a dumbbell in each hand, raised to your chest, keeping them shoulder-width apart. Extend your arms straight up from your body. Do not lock your elbows. Return your arms to your chest. Repeat.

Pushups

Pushups can serve as an alternative to presses because they work the same muscles. Begin by lying face down on the ground. Keeping your legs together, extend them straight out and keep your toes touching the floor. Position your hands flat on the floor right above your chest. Keep your back straight and make sure your core muscles are stabilized. Next, push your body up with your hands until the only body parts touching the ground are your hands and toes. Make sure your back stays straight. Slowly bring yourself back down to the ground until your nose touches the floor. Repeat.

Side Plank Star

The side plank star works your core muscles. Start out in a side plank position. Keeping your glutes, abs and lower back tight, raise your top leg as high as you can so that your body assumes a star shape. Bring your leg back down and then repeat. After ten repetitions, roll over onto the other side and repeat the process.

Chapter 5: Diet and Nutrition for Basketball Players

For many basketball players, the difference being a good player and an ultimate player is diet and nutrition. Star players need muscular bodies that have a low amount of body fat to be able to efficiently maneuver on the court. Without a strong diet and nutrition plan, it can be difficult to maintain a muscular body with less than fifteen percent of body fat.

Protein

Protein is an important nutrient that can help you stay energized and slim because it boosts your metabolism while building muscle. This, in turn, enables your body to eradicate fat and build body tissue. Workouts cause the fibers in your muscles to tear. Protein consumption can help repair them, a process that involves building additional muscle fiber. On average, a basketball player should ingest at least twenty grams of protein in every meal. Another way to calculate your daily protein needs is to eat one gram per pound of your body weight. Instead of eating food that claims to contain protein, such as protein bars, you should get your intake from real food sources. Some of the best sources are chicken, fish, eggs, turkey, Greek yogurt, and nuts. Additionally, you can drink a protein shake a half hour after each workout, to give your muscles some energy to jumpstart the rebuilding process.

Here are some more great sources for protein:

- Dairy products, such as milk, yogurt and cheese

- Lean beef, such as top sirloin or top round steak

- Legumes

Carbohydrates

Unlike protein, which you should consume in a steady amount each day, it is better to adjust your intake of carbohydrates based on your daily activity. Think of your carbohydrate intake as putting gas in a car; if you drive the car all day, you will need to fill it completely but if the car is parked all day, you will only need to replace what evaporates.

Just as gas provides the "energy" your car needs to drive, carbohydrates provide your body with the fuel you need to stay energized. If you have a heavy workout planned for the day you'll need more carbohydrates than on a light workout day or a rest day. Consuming too many carbohydrates on a light day may encourage your body to store the energy as extra body fat, extra deadweight you really don't need to lug around on the court.

However, not all carbohydrates are alike. it is important to avoid simple carbohydrates (white bread, candy, energy drinks, etc.) and aim for complex carbohydrates such as those found in fruits and vegetables. About thirty minutes to an hour and a half before a heavy workout, eat a small amount of complex carbohydrates that are slow to digest; afterwards consume a 2:1 ratio of carbohydrates to protein. For example, if you eat 25 grams of protein then you should eat 50 grams of carbohydrates. If your workout is light, only consume a 1:1 ratio. These carbohydrates will digest faster causing a boost to anabolism and insulin.

Here are some excellent complex carbohydrate sources:

- Leafy green vegetables
- Kale
- Broccoli
- Cauliflower
- Onions
- Bell Peppers
- Apples
- Bananas
- Berries
- Tomatoes
- Avocados
- Citrus fruits
- Whole wheat bread
- Whole wheat pasta
- Oats

- Bran
- Rye
- Beans
- Rice
- Potatoes

Fats

Fats are typically looked down upon, but the right fats are actually helpful. Fat can be detrimental in excessive amounts. However, the "healthy" fats, monounsaturated and polyunsaturated fats, should make up twenty percent of your total calories and can help you maintain your energy levels. It is best to consume your daily intake of fats in the morning so that you can maintain your energy level throughout the day. Avoid trans fats, saturated fats and hydrogenated fats like the plague.

Here are some sources for healthy fats:

- Nuts and seeds
- Fish
- Fish oil
- Peanut butter
- Avocados
- Olives
- Extra virgin olive oil

Hydration

Keeping hydrated is a top priority for any sport, including basketball. Hydration helps you feel healthy and energized while keeping your metabolism elevated and maintaining your body temperature. Your daily water consumption should consist of at least eighty ounces, though if you work out hard under a hot sun, you should drink even more. Your urine can serve as a hydration indicator. Dark urine indicates that you are not hydrated enough and should drink more water. Clear urine suggests that you are properly hydrated. Sports drinks are good for hydration but it is recommended that you dilute them halfway with water to reduce the sugar content. You can help your body remain hydrated by consuming fruits and vegetables, but these should already be a regular part of your diet.

Tips for Staying Healthy and Energized

- Supplements can help if you have a chronic deficiency or food allergies, but you should never rely on them to replace your intake of vitamins and minerals. You should provide your body with the nutrients you need through real food. If you choose, you can take a multivitamin to make sure you don't have any deficiencies. Only use protein powder in your post-workout shakes.

- Eat breakfast every day. When you wake up, it is important to provide nutrients to your muscles, since you have not eaten overnight. Breakfast with a high amount of protein can help you keep body fat off because if you go too long without eating, your body will begin to store energy as fat. Your breakfast should contain at least twenty grams of protein and does not have to be extravagant; you can eat yogurt with fruit, wheat toast with almond butter or a vegetable egg omelet, for example.

- Set aside adequate time to prepare your food. One of the main reasons all people, not just athletes, rely on fast food or frozen microwavables is a lack of time for food preparation. However, if you believe it's important enough, you will *make* the time for food prep.

    Look at it this way. You've hear it said, "you are what you eat." This is true. The more chemicals you ingest as part of those pre-packaged meals, the more toxins you will be carrying around instead of energizing nutrients. Preparing your own food is the only way you can ensure that you are eating from the best sources and avoiding life-destroying trans fats and simple carbohydrates that can work against your plan for ultimate fitness.

- An easy way to find food prep time is to consider it a part of your workout. For every three hours you spend working out, give yourself one hour in the kitchen. Since food is a huge part of keeping your body fit, it makes sense to consider this as part of your workout routine. You can create some healthy pre-packaged foods, especially snacks, by taking one block of time to buy large containers of healthy snacks and packaging them into individual portions so they're easy grab and go.

    Another option is to take one block of several hours out of your week to go grocery shopping and cook a bulk amount of food that you can package individually. Put single portions in storage containers that you can grab and heat up. Freeze a few containers so you aren't stuck eating the same thing all week. The next week make something different, again freezing a few containers, so that eventually you'll have a variety in the freezer from which to choose as well as your fresh batch. Just pull items out of the freezer the day before you plan to eat them, so they have time to thaw.

Chapter 6: Building Mental Strength

Building mental toughness is the first step toward sharpening your mind on the court. Once you have reached peak mental toughness you will rarely catch yourself believing that something is impossible. You will have just what it takes to reach your maximum potential. Mental toughness will enable you to focus on your most important goals with a calm mind, even if you are under a great deal of competitive pressure. The more you rehearse mock scenarios and practice affirming statements, the more your confidence and self-worth will grow, until your mind is functioning at its ultimate strength! Mental toughness doesn't usually develop naturally; it is up to you to develop it thoroughly.

Mental toughness involves a combination of confidence-building tactics and the honing of your sense of self-worth. Practice putting yourself into mock challenges to increase your inner resilience. This actually works, because our minds are unable to differentiate between a real situation and a practice one.

Here are a few confidence-building tips:

- You can simulate a high-pressure scenario during your practice. Decide how you want to handle the circumstances and practice executing your response. Focus on your execution of tasks steering your mind away from the feeling of being pressured.

- Pay attention to your body language. Negative body language opens the door to a poor attitude. It also sends a message to your opponents that you are vulnerable. As you train yourself to be aware of your body language on the court you are conditioning your posture to portray calm confidence. Your strong posture communicates to your brain that you *are* confident; eventually you will actually believe this message!

- Keep your eyes on the court and not on the audience. Your mind will follow your eyes.

- Another helpful strategy is to ask your coach or a teammate to yell out a phrase, such as, "You can do it!", whenever they see your focus starting to slip. You can train yourself to recognize this phrase as a trigger to refocus your mind.

The rest of the techniques in this chapter will help you develop and build your mental strength and toughness so you can become an all-star basketball player.

Build Your Confidence

You must own self-confidence before you can become a great athlete. Your confidence level often determines your ability to achieve your goals. The more confidence you have, the more likely you will be to succeed. You can have all the physical strength and endurance in the world, but you must also have a level of trust in your abilities. If you believe you can make a three-point shot then there's nothing to keep you from making it! If you don't, then your chances of making it may be pretty scarce.

There are things you can do to build your confidence. Many of these techniques are simple. Some easy ways to boost your self-confidence include standing tall, dressing well, practicing speaking in front of the mirror, and practicing positive self-affirmations.

Another way to build confidence is to surround yourself with a strong support system. Since basketball is a team sport, you have a ready-made support system in your teammates. As you promote and build each other up, you will both enhance your on-court teamwork and build your personal confidence level.

A positive attitude can also help you achieve and maintain a strong level of confidence. Positive thinking does not just happen, however. It is a conscious moment-by-moment choice to view the glass not only as half-full, but refillable.

Here are a few more confidence-building tips that go hand-in-hand with basketball:

- Your core foundation for confidence is laid by strength training, exercising, and eating healthy. Of course, these contribute to your basketball skills and physical conditioning as well.

- Know how to use the 80/20 rule to your advantage. Basically, this rule suggests you should focus on the twenty percent of your game that will increase your results the most. For example, if you are an otherwise well-rounded player whose weakness is running, focusing on your running can help improve your overall game by up to eighty percent.

- Mentally replay moments that caused you to feel great. People with low self-esteem tend to wallow in negative past experiences, which only leaves them feeling like any effort will lead to further failure. By thinking through times when you felt most alive and most successful, you remind yourself that you are indeed capable of greatness!

- When you catch yourself thinking negatively, tell yourself, "Stop!" out loud if you can. Then consciously turn your imagination toward anything positive.

- Meditation is a powerful way to help yourself direct your thoughts and learn how to control them. It is easy and can be practiced anywhere, as long as the place is relatively peaceful and you are comfortable with what you're wearing. Meditation can be refreshing to your mind and can really help you harness your confidence.

Find Self-Awareness

Self-awareness can help pave your road to success as an athlete. True self-awareness enables you to embrace both your strengths and your weaknesses, to recognize your talents and your flaws. Athletes often find it hard to come to terms with self-awareness in the presence of their coaches, because they don't like to admit their faults to the person who controls their time on the court. However, frank honesty with yourself and before those who support you can help improve your skills, develop useful playing habits, and may well boost your overall self-confidence.

One way to begin is to set an accountability goal for the next two weeks. I have found that a good way to do this is to keep a progress journal. In this journal, I write down every positive and negative experience I have known in my career.

When you do this, write about how good you feel about yourself and how it has made you a stronger athlete. When you describe a negative experience, write about what went wrong, what you learned from the experience, and how you plan to deal with this the next time it crops up. The best part about keeping all of this in a journal is that it is fun to go back and review from time to time to see how far you've come.

Define Your Goals as an Athlete

Without setting goals, you are very likely to never achieve success. Your goals serve as the roadmap that keeps you on track. Without goals, you are more likely to veer off course and lose track of what you need to do to become a great basketball player. Here are some helpful tips that can get you started on goal-setting:

- **Make goals a habit.** To be motivated for anything, it is essential to set specific goals and know what you're going to do to reach them. Without goals, it is very hard to intelligently steer your life in the direction desire.

- **Review your goals.** The first thing you can do to keep motivated in your athletic career is to set goals and review them several times a day. Write down on paper exactly what you are shooting for. Post them in a prominent place where you will see them every day. Then make it a practice to read them aloud several times a day.

- **Put your goals in writing.** When you write something down, you tend to retain it much better. Take a few minutes right now to write down some goals, if you haven't yet done this. Start each goal with the phrase "I will easily-" For example, you could say, "I will easily work out four times each week." Frame your goals in a way that you will know when you've reached them; that is, make them clearly defined, measureable, and realistically achievable. Paint a verbal picture that is compelling and is something that really excites you. Too many people set small goals that don't mean much to them. Don't be afraid to dream big and to shoot for something truly incredible.

- **Create a plan of action**. Having goals is great, but if you don't know how to work toward them, you will more than likely never reach them. Break down your long-term goals into series of short-term goals. This is one way to develop an action plan. Short-term goals, also called sub-goals make your journey easier and more manageable.

  The process is fairly straightforward. Write a long-term goal, then break it down into realistic, achievable steps toward that goal. Let's say that one of your goals is to implement a new eating plan that will better enhance your performance. You've got your goal—now think about what you can do to improve your eating habits. One strategy could be to clean out your cupboards and get rid of anything that doesn't support your new objective. Another application would be to research healthy meals for athletes.

- **Read your goals** at least once a day and review your current action steps throughout the day. This will help keep you focused and motivated to make progress. Any time you find yourself feeling unmotivated, refer back to your goals and review the action plan that will get you there.

- **Figure out why your goals matter.** By asking yourself why you want to reach each goal, you can be reminded of your true purpose. The power behind asking, "Why?" lays a foundation for motivation, which is the engine behind achieving success.

- Reward yourself. Some people do not need a tangible reward to find satisfaction. They are motivated to do something just for the enjoyment it brings them or others. But if you're not full of inner motivation to forego that triple mocha latte, an action plan can impose an external motivator, especially if you couple achieving an objective with a desirable reward.

Visualize Success

Basketball is a very physical sport that requires physical capability. But with any sport, success is not just handed to you. You must have an inner desire that will carry you through the tough times (and all successful people have gone through tough times) to make it to the top. In addition to setting goals it helps if you visualize yourself achieving them.

Visualization is a powerful technique to feed your motivation and ultimately, achieve success. Think about what you want and why you want it. Then, think about what your life will be like once you've got it. For example, if you are working hard as a college basketball player, think about how great your life will be once you've signed your first deal with a professional league and are driving an expensive car and living in a mansion. Your specific visualization will be different, based on your individual goals and what's important to you.

Visualization is something the top pros in the world do on a consistent basis. My advice is to make visualization a habit you practice every day to dramatically increase your chances of success. In addition to visualizing the details of performing flawlessly, envision the scene as if you were ten to fifteen feet away in the third person, observing yourself. Just allow the scene to flow naturally with you doing everything perfectly to achieve your desired goal.

Affirm your Success

You can combine visualization with positive self-statements for an even more powerful effect. Everybody thinks negative thoughts sometimes. It is human nature. However, continual positive self-statements can combat those thoughts. Since negative thoughts are so common, you cannot get rid of them completely. Instead, you can use positive words and phrases to effectively overwhelm negativity with positive affirmations. For example, instead of thinking, "Training is tiring me out so badly that I just want to give up," think, "The work is making me a better player. Plus, it'll help me sleep well tonight."

Avoid comparisons.

It is easy to compare yourself to others and think how bad – or how good – you play compared to them. Get those thoughts out of your head right now. Both pride and defeatism distract you from the task at hand. They will ultimately interfere with your playing and prevent you from performing at your very best. Instead, set your sights on your game plan and your winning strategies.

No More Excuses

Excuses are a big reason that many athletes fall into the groove of becoming unmotivated and unsuccessful. When you continually make excuses for why you are not progressing toward your goals, you will likely never achieve success. A good way to trap an excuse in the making is when you hear yourself saying, "but." Whenever you feel that word rolling off your tongue, clap your mouth shut and don't let it out.

For example, if you hear yourself saying, "I want to keep my energy levels consistent, *but* I really want to eat these french fries", immediately recognize this "but" as an excuse for not sticking to your goal. One way to counter this tendency is to use reverse psychology on your excuses. For example, you could say, "I really want to eat those french fries *but* if I do that, I won't reach my goal of becoming a basketball powerhouse."

Practice Focused Breathing

If you cannot help but feel anxious before a game, one helpful strategy is to practice focused breathing. Focused breathing enables you to beat anxiety and manage the stress you are feeling. When we are tense or angry we tend to hold our breath. Focused breathing counters that tendency; the process of controlled breathing requires some core muscles to relax, encouraging your mind to relax as well. It can keep you from losing your cool and blowing a big opportunity with unseemly behavior.

The more you practice this strategy, the more naturally it will come to you. While it is best practiced when you are in a quiet place at home, you can implement focused breathing in the middle of a game when you feel anxiety or anger rising. This is where practice will pay off. With your first inhale, your mind and body will connect back to the peaceful relaxation you experience when you do this at home. Past practice can actually help you relax in the middle of a noisy tense environment

Here is how to perform focused breathing:

- Get comfortable but stand or sit with a straight spine.

- Take in a long, slow breath through your nose.

- As you inhale, visualize your stomach filling up with air.

- Hold your breath for three seconds.

- While counting to six, slowly breathe out through your mouth and visualize all the negative emotions leaving your body.

- Repeat this visualization several times, then perform several more breaths as you visualize positive thoughts and enlivening energy entering with each inhale and permeating every cell in your body with each exhale.

Develop a Performance Ritual

Many successful athletes develop a performance ritual to help them prepare for a major performance. A ritual is a series of steps you take before a "big moment" to help you get into the right mental and emotional state of mind. There are two ways to utilize a performance ritual: beforehand and during the moment. In basketball, players get multiple breaks in between periods and between stints on the court, so you can use that time to focus on your in-the-moment ritual. What you include in your ritual and how you perform it is entirely up to you, but here are a few popular things that many athletes include in their rituals:

Before the game:

- Eat a meal at a pre-planned time.
- Double-check your equipment.
- Visualize your end success.
- Scope out the venue you'll be playing in.
- Wear clothes that boost your self-esteem.
- Record and re-watch your best games.
- Spend some quiet time with yourself

During the game:

- Perform some stretches to distract yourself from negative emotions.
- Visualize your success.
- Speak with your coach.
- Employ positive self-talk.
- Speak with players who are supportive.

Once you have figured out your personal performance ritual, create a game plan in which you put it all together and try it out. Have a few alternatives activities in the back of your head in case what you're doing doesn't work out. Try to keep a consistent pre-game time schedule so you don't find yourself rushing or anxious about your circumstances. Both hurry and anxiety are counterproductive to calm awareness and quiet confidence.

Develop Emotional Control

Competitive sports, with personal image at stake, can tax the character of the most easy-going athlete. The stresses of the game can make it extremely difficult for highly competitive athletes to maintain control of their emotions. It is not uncommon for an athlete to lose his or her cool after making a mistake or being on the receiving end of a bad call from the referee. However, when you lose your temper on the court, it can really ruin your reputation. Audience members, other players, and your coaches may view you as immature or easily distracted. A tantrum can also cost you playing time and if too disruptive can cost your team if you are penalized. One way to prevent yourself from losing your cool is to develop your emotional control.

Jim Loeher, a sports psychologist, has developed four emotional markers of mental toughness. Awareness of these markers can help you develop emotional control:

- Emotional Flexibility – The ability to act calmly under pressure in a range of situations as well as the ability to display a variety of positive emotions.

- Emotional Responsiveness – The ability to stay emotionally involved in a competitive situation.

- Emotional Strength – The ability to maintain emotional objectivity in any situation and to continue to fight (not with your fists, but toward your objective).

- Emotional Resiliency – The ability to quickly recover from a setback.

There are many things you can do to develop emotional control. First, develop a strategy to help you regain composure after experiencing an event that affects your emotions. To do this, you must be able to recognize what causes you to lose your cool. In most cases, it is because you find yourself not living up to your high expectations of yourself. Other common causes include being worried about what others think of you, negative self beliefs, and the fear of failure.

One way to head off an emotional meltdown is to use the three Rs: Recognize, Regroup and Refocus. First, you must recognize your warning signs that a meltdown is imminent. Secondly, you dispute your negative emotions by regrouping your thoughts. For example, if you find your emotions are stirred up by a specific negative statement, nullify it by thinking of an equal and opposite positive statement. Then you must refocus, which means getting your mind back into the present to focus on the game at hand. Ask yourself what you can focus on to help your team.

Focus on the Here and Now

It is important for athletes to be able to focus in the present moment in order to attain peak performance in games. During a typical game, an athlete's concentration tends to come and go. The key is to increase your total concentration until it encompasses a whole game. When you are in total concentration, your focus is on the game alone and time becomes irrelevant (except for the shot clock and the game clock, of course). Total concentration enables you to ignore distractions like negative thoughts, or if they intrude, to refocus quickly. The three Rs can help here.

Your ability to concentrate for increasingly long durations will only come with practice over time. You can practice extending your concentration during scrimmages as well as games. Practice achieving total concentration with the help of the three Rs prior to playing a big game so that when the time comes, you can more easily concentrate on winning.

Overcome Mental Obstacles

No matter how long you've been a basketball player, you will sometimes come face to face with a mental obstacle. The more confident you are, the easier it is to overcome one, but sometimes they still manage to get you down. Mental obstacles often consist of negative thoughts, self-talk and beliefs that can hold you back from playing at your peak capacity. The ability to overcome mental obstacles will help you remain strong through every situation you encounter, both as a basketball player and throughout your life.

One way to overcome a negative mental obstacle is to look for the positive within. For example, a player who is sidelined with an injury may have negative feelings of being unable to move or function normally or spend time with his team. This often leads to "woe is me" feelings. However, there are positive aspects to down time. Time off can allow overworked muscles to rest. It can give you space to reflect on where you are and where you want to go with your life. You also have been given the gift of detachment, enabling you to watch the game, free from the pressure of keeping yourself mentally geared up to play. As you watch your teammates, you can learn things about them that will increase your ability to interact productively on the court in the future. You can gain insights as a "spectator" that you would never receive as a player.

Another example of overcoming a mental obstacle is when a player experiences a defeat. This can easily lead to negative self-talk and "woe is me" self-pity. However, there are positives, even in this situation. Even failure can be analyzed and learned from. This is how you turn a shameful, painful experience into an advantage. Guaranteed, you are not likely to walk unprepared into *that* situation again! You'll be much better prepared to succeed next time.

Some athletes find themselves nervous before a big game, even if they are highly experienced or famous. Nerves are common; paired with a lack of confidence nerves have the power to capsize your performance, no matter how good you are. Performance anxiety can cause muscles to become rigid and nonresponsive. It can result in difficulties breathing; it can upset your stomach and cause your heart to race. Mentally, it can lead to a loss of focus as your anxious mind bounces from one disastrous imagination to the next.

To beat performance anxiety, you must be able to identify these feelings and, avoid becoming anxious about them. Embrace your performance anxiety. Nerves are how your body gears up for what it perceives as danger. Those pre-game jitters are evidence that your adrenaline is building up in preparation for a fight-or-flight scenario.

You have a choice. You can let your nerves get you down, turning your legs into quivering jelly and the rest of you into a blubbering basket case. Or...you can choose to embrace those nerves and harness all that nervous energy for the ride of your life! Instead of a basket case, you become basketball itself.

When you feel your nerves rising, this is the time to talk to yourself. Really. Tell yourself why you're here and what you're going to accomplish today. Visualize every aspect of your game. Just as you practice layups, free throws, footwork, passing, etc., practice mentally imagining every detail of your game. Walk through everything, from the moment you step out onto the court, hear your name announced, and listen to the crowd's support. Internally watch yourself make flawless layups and three-point shots, dribble circles around your opponents, snap the ball to your teammates, and strip the ball from the opposing players. Visualize yourself perfectly executing even the plays you consider the most difficult. Let yourself feel excited about how well you are playing. This will convert all that nervous energy into playing power. Then go on and play your heart out, knowing you have more than enough oomph to accomplish anything and everything that will be required of you in this game.

When it comes to mental success in a sport, sometimes it is not always about who is the fastest or most powerful but who has the strongest positive attitude.

Do Not Fear Competition or Failure

Fear is an emotion that everybody experiences, not just athletes. However, for athletes, fear can hold them back from achieving their dreams. Fear of failure can hold you back, but you can also utilize it to drive you toward your goals. Don't let yourself fear failure itself. If the fear of failure prevents you from even trying, then it is holding you back. If the fear of failure causes you to think of what kind of person you want to be in the future, it can drive you forward.

For example, let's say you'd like to be the provider for your family and be able to afford nice things, including a house in a nice neighborhood. Your goal is to do this by becoming a well-paid, professional athlete. In this case, your image of failure is the inability to provide for your family. You fear this, so it drives you to achieve your goal. If you fear failure itself, you will likely not even try to become a professional athlete out of sheer embarrassment, thus eliminating this as a way to become an effective provider for your family.

Learn to Handle Rejection.

Rejection is inevitable. At one point or another in your life you will be turned down. It matters little whether you're rejected from a sports team, a college, a job, a marriage, or anything else. It's easy to let rejection discourage you, but if you can view even rejection in a positive light, you will be much better off as you travel through life.

If you are rejected from something, view it as an opportunity to learn, grow, and improve. There's no need to get all emotional if someone gives you criticism (which is another form of rejection). Most critics are just trying to help. If you can learn to receive criticism without blowing your lid, then you will be much better off in your journey through life.

Conclusion

I hope this book was able to help you discover what you can do in order to be a better basketball player. Basketball is a great sport to play but, as you have learned throughout this book, it requires a great deal of commitment, determination, and hard work. First, you must master the fundamental skills of dribbling, shooting, passing, etc. Then you must fully understand how to stretch, warm-up and physically train for ultimate speed, strength, endurance, and explosiveness on the court. Your nutritional needs are essential to your body's ability to perform. Finally, you must have what it takes mentally to become a great player. When combined with physical skill, mental strength can turn you into a basketball powerhouse.

Your next step is to figure out where you are in your game. Are you new to basketball or are you already an experienced player? If you're new, you may need to start by studying the rules and the terminology of the game to fully understand it. If you already know these details, your next step is figuring out what area(s) need your focus on the most: technical skills, physical training, working on your diet, or mental toughness. I recommend putting together a customized physical training plan first, as a skeletal framework. Upon this framework you can then hang the details of technical skills and proper nutrition, along with mental toughness. A 30 day plan usually works best, and after you have mastered 3 or 4 new skills then move on to the other things you would like to improve upon. Be sure to be consistent, journal your progress and harness a positive mindset and you are bound to notice good things happening to your game as the weeks go by.

Finally, if you discovered at least one thing that has helped you or that you think would be beneficial to someone else, be sure to take a few seconds to easily post a quick positive review. As an author, your positive feedback is desperately needed. Your highly valuable five star reviews are like a river of golden joy flowing through a sunny forest of mighty trees and beautiful flowers! *To do your good deed in making the world a better place by helping others with your valuable insight, just leave a nice review.*

My Other Books and Audio Books
www.AcesEbooks.com

Peak Performance Books

Health Books

Be sure to check out my audio books as well!

 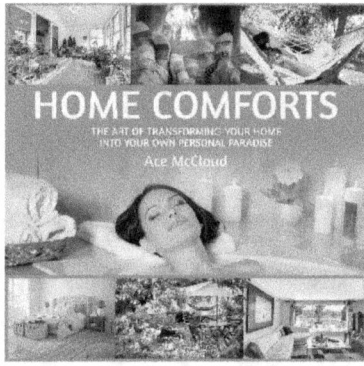 

Check out my website at: **www.AcesEbooks.com** for a complete list of all of my books and high quality audio books. I enjoy bringing you the best knowledge in the world and wish you the best in using this information to make your journey through life better and more enjoyable! **Best of luck to you!**